We dedicate this book to everyone who wants to explore the potential of what living miracles can achieve.

Thank you to each of our children: Blake, Maeve and Matty, for inspiring us and helping us grow daily.

Am I A Rabbit?
The Liberation Of Fear

Dr. Kristin Heins, ND
& Marc Finkelstein

So many things can seem spooky and strange.

Feeling fear, or not, is something you can change.

When you see the world only for its harms,

You will certainly miss out on some of its charms.

Rabbits are cute but their fears do the same.

A cuddle from kids they surely won't get.

They won't make new friends or share any food.

They are acting on fear and not to be rude.

Unlike you, a rabbit takes no time to think.

They act only on impulse, and respond in a blink.

Fear makes them freeze up or hop away quick.

It was just a balloon popping, at the picnic.

Your brain allows you to THINK before acting.

Understanding your **fear** before reacting.

It's true some things make sense to avoid,

Like wrestling a shark...

Or riding an asteroid.

Can you find **any** proof and make a list?

✓ I HAVE NEVER HEARD A MONSTER

✓ I HAVE NEVER SMELLED A MONSTER

✓ I HAVE NEVER SEEN A MONSTER

Reasons not to be scared help you move through your fright,

And instead allow you to sleep through the night.

Don't assume the worst when it is untrue.

See instead what is there,
right in front of you.

25

Like trying the slide that you find so high,

With your mom at the bottom saying "please try".

Living scared like a rabbit is a sad way to be.

28

Think through the fear
and you will be free.

Children greatly rely on socialization and the media as they develop self identity, values, and normative behavioural responses. Many years can be spent in discord and struggle before children discover the freedom that can exist when finding and acting their true selves.

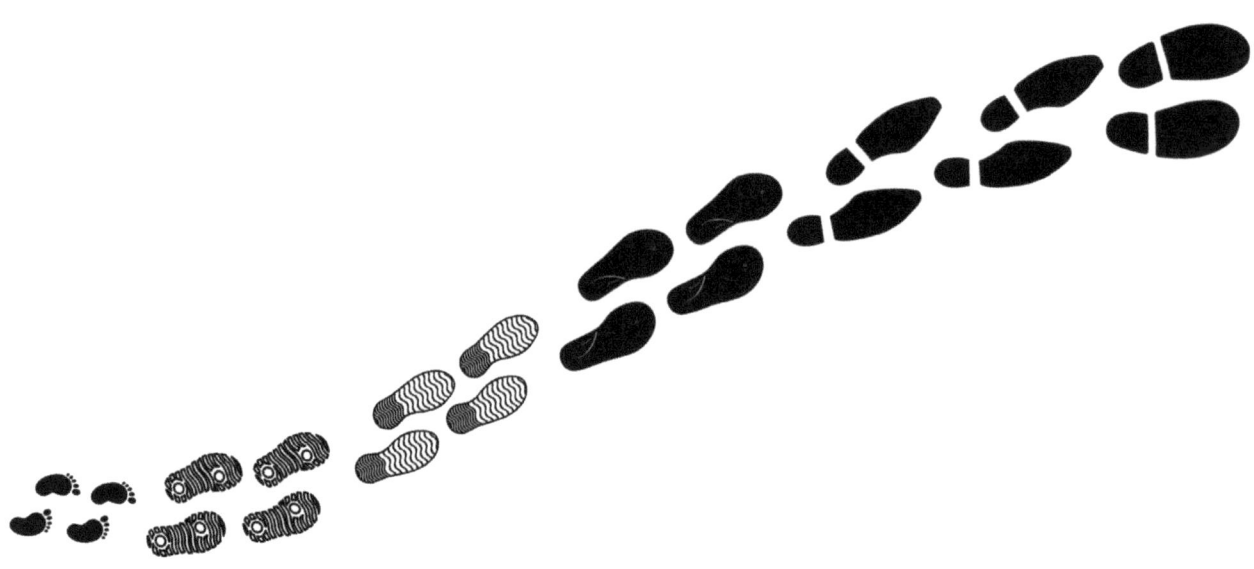

Through this series, and with the help of their caregivers and educators, children can more easily understand authenticity and personal mastery, both introspectively and within the world around them.

Kristin is a naturopathic doctor who has been studying humanistic and relational psychotherapy for the past decade and currently works under clinical supervision.

Marc is a PhD (candidate) in Decision Science, author and specialist in behavioural science.

Both authors are parents, and are passionate about nurturing the life skills necessary for children (and their caregivers) to bravely be the people they are.

Many thanks to the creative team for helping to bring these books to life.

© 2017 Marc Finkelstein & Kristin Heins

All rights reserved. This book or parts thereof may not be reproduced in any form, stored in any retrieval system, or transmitted in any form by any means—electronic, mechanical, photocopy, recording, or otherwise—without prior written permission of the publisher, except as provided by law. For permission requests, write to the publisher, at the address below.

Published worldwide by
Masala Enterprises Limited
1400 - 52 Lawrence Avenue West
Toronto, ON M5M 1A4

www.masalaenterprises.ca

For information about purchasing in bulk, educational needs, professional needs, or other special orders, contact Masala Enterprises at 1-866-999-2907 or sales@masalaenterprises.ca.

Book series information:
www.WhoAmIBooks.ca

Hardcover: 978-1-7752179-8-5 | Paperback: 978-1-7752179-7-8 | eBook: 978-1-7752179-6-1

www.ingramcontent.com/pod-product-compliance
Lightning Source LLC
Chambersburg PA
CBHW041715160426
43209CB00018B/1843